NICK DRAKE

THE FAREWELL GLACIER

BLOODAXE BOOKS

ISBN: 978 1 85224 933 5

First published 2012 by
Bloodaxe Books Ltd,
Highgreen,
Tarset,
Northumberland NE48 1RP.

www.bloodaxebooks.com
For further information about Bloodaxe titles
please visit our website or write to
the above address for a catalogue.

Supported by
**ARTS COUNCIL
ENGLAND**

Cover design: Neil Astley & Pamela Robertson-Pearce.

Printed in Great Britain by
Bell & Bain Limited, Glasgow, Scotland.

For Edward Gonzalez Gomez

Out of whose womb came the ice?
And the hoary frost of heaven, who hath gendered it?
The waters are hid as with a stone
And the face of the deep is frozen
  BOOK OF JOB XXXVIII 29-30

You have to begin to change your mind to understand the Arctic
  BARRY LOPEZ

We must travel in the direction of our fear
  JOHN BERRYMAN

ACKNOWLEDGEMENTS

I would like to thank David Buckland and Cape Farewell for inviting me to join their expedition to Svalbard in September 2010. This poem grew out of that voyage. Images, blogs and information are available on the websites www.capefarewell.com and www.nickfdrake.com.

Many thanks to Deborah Warner for permission to reproduce her beautiful photograph on the cover; to Robert Davies of the Polar Poetry Circle for his fine responses to drafts of the poem; and to Matt Clark of United Visual Artists for his commission to create a poem for UVA's *High Arctic* installation at the National Maritime Museum (2011-12).

The National Maritime Museum was a supportive and enthusiastic home for the installation; I would especially like to thank Kevin Fewster, Kevin Sumption, Richard Ferguson, and all those who worked on *High Arctic*, particularly the volunteers.

Of all the books about the Arctic which I read in the London Library stacks, Barry Lopez's *Arctic Dreams: Imagination and Desire in a Northern Landscape* (Harvill Press, 1999) was the greatest discovery. I would like to acknowledge my debt to him here.

Many thanks to John Mole and to Jackie Kay for comments, insight and encouragement. Also to Anna Madeley and Geoffrey Streatfeild for their recording of the poem for *High Arctic*, and to Walter Donohue, Max Eastley and Henrik Ekeus.

Thanks also to the other guests and crew of the *Noorderlicht* – Sonia van Berkel, Simon Boxall, Ted Broeckhuyse, Kevin Buckland, Mikhail Durenkov, Deborah Iglesias Rodriguez, Iris Haeussler, Cynthia Hopkins, Nina Horstmann, Beth Kapusta, Ruth Little, Paul Miller, Marina Moskvina, Daria Parkhomenko, Rentske Ritzema, Joy Shumake-Guillemot, Leonid Tishkov, Andrey Volkov, Matt Wainwright and Aafke van der Werf.

PREFACE

I travelled to Svalbard with Cape Farewell in September 2010. We sailed aboard the *Noorderlicht*, a glorious late 19th-century sailboat, and explored the west and north of the archipelago for three weeks. We were no more than 600 miles from the North Pole. What had been maps and dreams became a deeply beautiful place that still felt like a dream world. It exists at both the scale of the enormous and ancient (glaciers, fjords, mountains) and the tiny and transient (the glorious miniature wonderland of the summer tundra). Time happens differently there; in late September, the end of the Arctic summer, the sun takes hours to set; darkness is brief. Light flies constantly into the eye from every direction, reflected and amplified and refracted by ice and water and sky. Silence rules – in the moments when we stopped walking and talking, it unfolded for miles all around us, and all we could hear was the static in our heads. It's also a confronting, powerful place, as we discovered the day the ship became stuck in pack ice the size of juggernauts, dragging us inexorably towards submerged rocks – while several polar bears gathered to observe.

It was a great privilege to visit the Arctic. This poem grew out of that experience, and the conversations with the scientists, artists and architects on board the *Noorderlicht*. We needed to understand how, as David Buckland writes, 'feverish human activity has impacted on the Arctic on a scale large enough to melt the Northern Ice Cap, and make glaciers disappear in decades. Scientific feedback loops exist in which changes accelerate and act on other systems to destabilise natural processes.' The science is complex; the truth of what's happening isn't. But it is confronting, in all sorts of ways.

The Farewell Glacier is conceived as one poem of many voices. I hope these voices – human and non-human – might talk to us, and each other, across time. There are many Arctics – indigenous, Canadian, Russian – but I wanted to trace the stories of the European exploration and exploitation of the Arctic, in all their curiosity, delight, greed, disaster, wonder, terror and euphoria, from the deep past, and into the near future because, as the Inuit say, *we are the people who have changed nature*. The Arctic holds a mirror up to us.

I have not attributed the voices on the page, as I wanted them to speak freely. Clues and further information about the voices can be found at the end of the book, and in the notes.

PART I

I sailed with the sun
Into a dream;
North past the sacred promontory
To the emporium called Belerion,
A land subject to frost
Where they shape tin from the mines
In the shape of a man's knucklebones;
North beyond the coast of Britannike
Into a strange summer;
The shadow of our mast
Lengthened across the sea each day;
In the diminished nights
New stars appeared, never before seen;
The pole star rose higher and higher –
Finally, after six days at sea, we saw
The lost land called Thule.
Theophrastus says time
Is an accident of motion
And surely what he says is true;
For we came to a place where the sun did not set,
And the ocean stopped,
And the waters congealed,
And the gnomon of our mast
Cast a shadow that reached to the horizon.
In the brief dark
I beheld *Arktikos*, the Great Bear,
The Pole Star
And the seven stars
Turning above my head
As if we were the still point
Of everything.

I staked my life and sailed into a dream;
When at last I returned home
They did not believe me.
I wrote the truth in a book,
But then the book was lost.
I am Phytheas, the Greek.
This was my dream.

*

We sailed in carraughs, long and narrow,
Made from willow
And tanned ox-hide caulked with tallow;
We sailed for seven years on the waves of creation
To reach the Isles of the Blessed,
The Garden of Eden,
Paradise –
Monks, pilgrims, latecomers, unbelievers and holy fools,
With wine and cold food, and heather for our bedding
So we slept on the sweet scent of home
In the nowhere of the sea.
Our anchor was a stone
Dropped in bays of silence
Where no man aged
For the sun held still in the sky.
We found an isle of birds
Singing Psalms and praising the Lord.
We came upon the Island of Laughter.
One day there appeared on the horizon
A crystal castle
Floating on the ocean;
We sailed towards it, and found,
Carved by the waves and the wind,
A passage through it;
And in that long light we stared
Into the eye of God.

*

I heard this story
From a man who had met a man
Whose name is forgotten
Or lost:

In the midst of the four countries I saw
A whirlpool into which there empties
The four indrawing seas that divide the North;
And the water rushes around and descends into the Earth
Just as if one were pouring it through a filter funnel,
Except that right under the Pole there lies
A bare rock in the midst of the Sea,
And it is all of magnetic stone
And it is as high as the clouds
And it is black and glistening
And nothing grows thereon
For there is not so much
As a handful of soil on it –
Four thousand souls have disappeared
On those indrawing seas
Since time began –
But I escaped to tell the tale
Of all I saw with my own eyes...

I plan to draw a projection
For the first time on any map
Of all he swore the man swore
Was true.

*

We sailed beyond knowledge
Into a great solitude;
The sea was grey glass;
The sails stiffened
And the deck and the rigging
Feathered with frost.

14

But we could go no further:
A horizon of white ice
Drove us into a storm;
The galley fire was quenched,
The men's hands were raw,
And the lookouts peered
Into a timeless blizzard –
Until we chanced upon the calm waters
We named Fair Haven.
Next day, we went ashore.
Uncountable barnacle geese
Observed us without fear
Until a volley of stones sent them
Crying into the sky;
We carried sixty eggs
Warm in the nests of our hands
Back to the ship, and cracked
And ate them.

We sailed south into a blue morning
But found ourselves trapped
Between two iron chains of hills;
Then the wind died, and the mist thickened;
Little auks and geese in the rocky cliffs
Shrieked their revenge,
For we were lost in the gloom;
But so were they, for they flew into our dead sails
And fell to the deck
Like an augury.

We escaped with our lives
And sailed east; but the ice
Took us in its grip;
Then a great darkness came –
But that is another story.

*

I am the only boy
On the *Amity*, sailed from Blackwall
In the spring
To the isle of Spitzbergen.
Captain Poole sent me on a skiff
Across the glassy waters;
I was ordered to set foot alone
On the barren shore.
The fog lifted and I turned
And saw mountains
In the sky.
The sun stayed still
And stared.
Among the stones I found
The horn of a reindeer.
I gave it to the captain
Who named the place
Horn Sound.
I am still there,
An old man
Standing at the edge of the world
In the silence in his head.

*

Fairhaven
Bell Point
Bell Sound
Ice Point
Ice Sound
Cross Road
Half Moon Island
Cape Cold
Horn Sound
Foul Sound
Low Sound
Comfortless Cove
Grim Mountain
Misery Mountain
Fog World
Black Point
Lost Point
Bird Song Rock

Where we disappeared

*

We came to shore on an island
I named Desolation;
We heard a lamentation
Like the war howl of wolves;
Strange men approached us
Across the waters;
So I called upon our gentlemen
To play their instruments, and to dance,
Alluring them by signs of courtesy.
One of them pointed to the sun
And then struck his breast so hard
All present heard the blow.
We offered them parts of our clothing
And continued to play and dance.
The next morning, we awoke to a drum
Beating from the same island;
This time they danced for us.
I found them void of craft or double-dealing.
And when we returned the following year
With additional backing from the City of Exeter,
They remembered us.
The light suffuses everything; this is
The place of greatest dignity on earth.

*

All that interminable day
Whales lay so thick about the ship
That some ran against our Cables
Some against the hull
And one against the Rudder.
One lay under our Beakhead
And slept there a long while.
Of what did he dream?
Not of this:
We did not need the shallops to pursue them.
They did not suspect us.

We flensed them with harpoons and knives
And boiled the blubber in copper kettles
And thence into casks.
Blood Sound. Stinking Sound.
I made dominoes from the bones.
We returned to London with 180 tons of oil
From seventeen whales and two walruses.
Now Amsterdam and San Sebastian
Dispatch their fleets.
It will be a war for industry.

I died two years after
Miserably and basely murdered
Between the sailor town of Ratcliff
On the north shore of the Thames,
And the towers of London.

*

High tide leaves the dead whale high and dry
On the stone beach;
Its prodigious mouth and lips are soft.
Under the chin, the skin is white.
We climb the blue-black hill of the body
To flense the creature with our knives,
And, as we work, we are to think of a Bible,
Black cover, vellum pages slit open, and the cracked spine
Running with blood.
In the merciless light
We sit in shifts and smoke our pipes
To mask the unholy reek and pong
Of the boiling, stinking oil of our great good fortune.
A summer's worth of barrels fill the holds.

We drink brandy
And grow afraid of the great silence
Always at our backs.
On Sundays we pray
To return home to our loved ones
In Hull and Peterhead and Aberdeen
And Dundee and Whitby and London.

From the industry of this Leviathan
Come candles and oil lamps,
Corset stays and the ribs of sunshades,
Collar-stiffeners and buggy-whips,
Paper-creasers and dominoes;
And even the future itself –
Light for the streets of cities
And fuel to drive the wheels of textile mills,
And eyeglass frames, chess pieces and piano keys.

But I left my bones
In the shallow graveyard of Dead Man's Island
In a narrow box of planks
Opened each winter by the curious frost.

*

Captain Jan Rijp;
I name this fjord, valley, glacier and river –
Rijpfjorden, Rijpdale, Rijpbreen and Rijpelva

But what about me, Thomas Edge,
Merchant and Whaler?
I name this island: Edgeland –

And we, the Basque whalers of St Jean de Luz
Name this headland
Biscayanland –

And what of us, the nameless men
Of Blubber Town on Broken Land –
The Kings of Nowhere?

Does anyone here remember
Who named Dead Man's Plain
And Comfortless Cove,

Misery Mountain, Half Moon Island,
Lost Point, Fog World
And Bird Song Rock?

*

Dreams of strange lands are all very well
But they must be financed
And made profitable, otherwise
Why go?
So I paid for Mr Frobisher and two ships
To find the passage to Cathay;
The Queen waved them farewell
From Greenwich Palace.
Yet when he returned, how did he repay me?
With stories –
Of no value to me.
But one of his sailors carried home a stone
Black as mystery
Merely for the sake of the place
From whence they came;
The assayers were unimpressed,
But I was in debt
And one was persuaded to agree the stone held gold.
From this flattery I raised new investment
To send ships back
To better recoup my investment;

This time the Queen permitted Frobisher
To kiss her hand,
And contributed a thousand pounds.
This time they brought 200 tons of stones
And the tusk of a sea-unicorn
Which was presented to her Majesty;
There was considerable dispute, I confess;
But on this I raised more finance,
Arranging for the ore to be assayed
At £5 per ton,
And sent back fifteen ships
Whose captains the Queen honoured
By permitting each to kiss her hand.
She placed a gold chain around Frobisher's neck
And named her new land
Meta Incognita.

One ship was lost. Forty men drowned.
The rest returned
With their holds filled with stones.
They were smelted
At Powder Mill Lane, Deptford,
And pronounced: *iron*.
Worthless.
I petition you for relief and assistance
From the Fleet Prison.
The iron will be salvaged
And turned into roads.

I only believe what I can hold in my hand.

*

Sing now, and raise the dead
Time for us to go
Sing now and raise the dead
Time for us to go

Ship after ship, year after year, century on century
Falling like snow on the black waves of the sea;
With stars, compasses, charts and reflecting quadrants
To measure our position in the Desolation

A long, long time, and a long time ago

Brave men, heroes, whalers, desperadoes,
Seafarers, mapmakers, explorers, audacious liars,
Thieves, renegades, gamblers, tellers of tall stories,
The tongue-tied, the truants, come rock and roll over

Sing now, and raise the dead
Time for us to go
Sing now and raise the dead
Time for us to go

For new markets, for fortune, for fame, for recognition,
For the fear of our fathers, for the love of our fathers,
For the pledge of our lovers, for the loss of our lovers,
For wages, for work, for better, for worse,

A long, long time, and a long time ago

We were bankrupted, shipwrecked, starved, blown down.
We ate candles and bird skin. We were drowned.
We were lost in the white cloud and never found.
We forgot our names. Our names were forgotten.

Sing now, and raise the dead
Time for us to go
Sing now and raise the dead
Time for us to go

We bought back stories no-one believed.
We bought back dreams we could not understand.
We were not understood. We found no words
In the failure of home for our stammering hearts –

Sing now and raise the dead
Time for us to go
Sing now and raise the dead
A long, long time ago

PART 2

This is what happened:
As the great Dark arrived,
I ordered a wagon cloth to be laid over the spars
For an exercise yard.
The men had their tasks. Cheerfulness
Was an order.
We performed plays on the Quarterdeck
And published the *North Georgia Gazette and Winter Chronicle*
Every Monday.
We caught a fox, named him Jack
And taught him to eat from our hands.
Carlo the white setter vanished
And was never seen again.
We baked bread daily, and brewed beer.
Mr Fisher poured water from the mast
To see if it would freeze
Before it hit the deck.
It is true we were never dry
And the thermometers cracked.
In the evenings the officers read
By the light of the blubber-oil lamps
And listened to music;
One on the flute, I on the violin.
The men were always busy with their tasks.
But all around us was the gloom
In which we took our walks
In darkness and deathlike silence
So different from the peaceable composure
Of a cultivated country;
We heard each other singing
A mile and more away.
I was twenty-nine years old.
I thought of Devon.
I stared at a stone in the snow for hours,
For pleasure,
And to calm my terror.

Some died of drink, some of madness.
Officers were ostracised.
Differences between officers
Led to the reading of the Articles of War
On the Quarter-deck.
I suppose that it not the story
You wish to hear.

When at last the sun returned
We wore black veils over our faces
Against the snow-light.
I saw halos and arcs;
A layer of light clouds passed under the sun revealing
Exquisite tints of lake, bluish green and yellow;
And a triple rainbow.

*

I was considering the works
Of reflection and refraction
When through my portable telescope
I observed an extraordinary appearance;
The mountains along that coast
Assumed the most fantastic forms
Of castles with lofty spires
And towers and battlements,
And I beheld them, as it were,
Metamorphose into great arches
And vast romantic bridges,
And the air itself was perfectly transparent –
I saw the land and ships
Enlarged and elevated,
Looming above the horizon –
The pure contrasts of black rock
And white snow
Drawing all together.

I contemplated a fogbow's
Bands of vivid colour;
The lower part of the circle
Descended beneath my feet
To the side of the ship
And although it could not be more
Than a hundred feet from my eye
It was perfect. And I saw
In the centre of that circle
A shadow, which was mine; my head
Conspicuously portrayed.
But my dear, why did I not see
In the nearness of eternity,
At that very moment
When I was contemplating
Shadows and light,
You were dying, so far away;
And what loomed over the horizon's lens
Was a distant and unknown future,
Which could not raise up
Ever again your living image
To my eyes?

*

One day differs very little from another;
We all turn out at eight and breakfast:
Hard bread, cheeses, corned beef,
Luncheon ham or Chicago tinned tongue,
Cod-caviar, anchovy roe; also
English ship biscuits with orange marmalade
Or Frame Food Jelly. As for beverages;
Coffee, tea or chocolate.
At one o'clock we assemble for dinner;
Soup, meat and dessert,
Or soup, fish and meat,
Or fish, meat and dessert.

Supper is almost the same
As breakfast. Outside
There are howlings and thunderings;
You feel the ice trembling
And rumbling under your feet;
In the semi-darkness
It splits in front of you –
A black gulf opens, and water streams up;
In every direction it is the same,
Stupendous thundering and roaring
With explosions like cannon salvos
Until the noise passes on and is lost
By degrees, in the distance.
Sitting here now alone
My thoughts involuntarily turn
To the year that has gone since we stood
And you threw the champagne against the bow
And the strong, heavy hull began to glide
So gently into the water. I held your hand,
Tears came to my eyes,
And I could not say a word.
All this is the continuation
Of what happened that joyful day;
But time is passing to no purpose;
We are stuck in a hole where the ice
Grinds round and round;
How long is it to last?
I eat, work, read, think, dream,
Go for a walk on the ice in the dark;
Below the horizon to the south
The sun is a dark red glow.
We are entering the long night of winter.
What will it bring us? Where shall we be
When the sun returns? No one can tell.
Shall I have nothing to write about
When I get home?

*

30

You will have heard the news, my love,
Of our disappearance;
You will know we are well supplied
With Chateaubriand steaks, and jams,
Monogrammed serviettes,
Lightweight aluminium cutlery
And Belgian chocolates.
You will know about our carrier pigeons
And the famous primus stove
That hangs outside the gondola
To cook our splendid dinners.
You will remember how Mr Andree announced
He would wear a dinner jacket
As a gesture of respect
For the formalities
In the wilderness –
And so he did.
You will not know the rest;
How, as our lovely balloon of Chinese pongee silk
Rose into the blue,
We left behind the drag ropes
By mistake; how we sailed
Into freezing fog, and could see nothing.
How the ice began to play with us,
Encrusting the silk, weighing it down;
And after 65 hours in the air
We sank onto the pack ice
And evacuated. We drank champagne
And ate biscuits and honey;
We dressed well in our socks
And fine Jaeger britches;
But you will not know
We cooked the tongues, kidneys and brains
Of polar bears, and fried blood-pancakes
With oatmeal and butter;
We toasted your birthday,
And strangely we were happy.
I took the photographs
Contained in these rolls

In this reflex camera, in its black sealed case,
And wrote this almanac
Of the great and the little things
For you, my love; perhaps
One day you will hold these lost
Negatives up to the daylight.
I think, after all, your love
Made a better balloon, of finer silk,
Of my heart; so I release it now,
Filled with one last breath
Into the air –

*

They called me the Iron Man
But there was a suspicious wooden feeling
In my feet.
When they sliced away my sealskin boots
Several of my toes
Snapped off at the joint,
Frozen.
I felt nothing.
For six weeks I lay
Not knowing if I would lose both feet.
In the end
I lost eight toes.
And then I carried on.

*

I remember
We set out in the light
Of midnight.
Step by step,
Foot by foot,
We made good progress
Across the ice
To the Pole's vicinity
Which he measured
With his sextant.
When I congratulated him on the achievement
He hid his face in his hands
And said nothing
To me.
If you look me up
In the indexes of your histories
I merit mention
As 'black manservant'
Or 'life-long associate',
Or not at all;
My black face
Invisible
In the snow
Of these white stories
That quarrel
For the victory of the Pole.
I was 'useful' –
For I spoke the language
Of the Eskimos,
I built sledges,
Drove dog teams
And was popular;
But still
I had to call him Sir.

I remember
I was the first man to stand
With 360 degrees beneath my feet
And east and west and north
Meaningless;
A black man
Out of Maryland
With our companions
Ootah and Ooqueah,
Egingwah and Seegloo,
Posed for the photograph
Holding flags
At the top of the world.

After I died
They put my black face
On a postage stamp
Worth 22c.
And then they moved my bones
To lie beside his
Who came to hate me,
In the Arlington National Cemetery.

*

They named me Ootah
And Odark
And Oodaaq
And Odaq
And Utaq.

Long after I died
They named an island after me;
The northernmost place in the world
Is a tiny territory,
A field of gravel
Less than 1 metre above sea level
At its highest point.

You can Google it.

*

When I was twelve
To win a bet
I walked across the thin ice of the frozen Severn
And never looked back.
Later, I resolved to walk
From Alaska to Svalbard
Across the sea ice
Via the Pole of Inaccessibility
And the North Pole.
My Inuit friends left a map
Pinned to the hut door
Marked with the places they thought I would die.
It was 3,800 miles;
We left in February,
Four men and forty dogs.
And in July we made camp
Because the ice was not drifting
In our favour.

When the sun returned
We continued through the next summer
To reach 90 degrees North.
I telegraphed the Queen.
Trying to stand on the pole
Was like trying to step
On the shadow of a bird
Circling overhead.
Two weeks later
A man took the first step on the Moon
And by the time we got home
We were forgotten.
You couldn't walk it now,
Even if you wanted to –
Why not?
Because the sea ice is melting,
And no one can walk on water.

PART 3

We were born in your dream of the future –
Released by fire
We ascended the winding stairs of the smoke stacks
Until we reached the orange sunrise
And the blue sky.
No one waved goodbye.
No one saw us go;
We were uncountable
And invisible.
One way or another
We were carried north
In the hands of the winds,
Through the stories of the rivers,
By the generosity of the oceans;
And when we arrived at the cold
Top of the world
It felt like home, sweet home;
And we waited in the long darkness
Until at last
The first light of the year transmuted us
Out of thin air and we came to rest
In ice and snow and black water.
Now we accumulate
And magnify
In the cells of fish, in the eggs of birds,
Inside the warm coats of seals and bears;
And in the wombs of mothers
We concentrate so the faces of the future
Take on our features,
And we sing our names into the ears
Of the unborn:
PCB; POP; DDT;
Caesium, technetium;
Mercury.

*

39

Aldrin
Bane
Brominated fire retardant
Carcinogenic aromatic hydrocarbons
Charm
Chlordane
Curse
Dibenzofurans
DDT
Dieldrin
Element
Emission
Endrin
Factor
Gobbledegook
Heptachlor
Hex
Hexachlorobenzene
Hocus Pocus
Hush Hush
Incognito
Jinx
Knock Knock
Lament
Lingo
Mercury
Mirex
Mutagenic
Noxious
Nonsense
Oracle
Polychlorinated biphenyls
Polycholrinated dibenzo-p-dioxins
Prayer
Quibble
Riddle
Scourge
Spell

Spook
Tetraogenic
Toxaphenic
Utter
Vex
Voodoo
Wrath
Execrate
Yabber
Yammer
Yatter
Zero

*

We are disturbed
By the light of day;
It sees through us,
Through the fine coils
Of our precise shells,
To the next-to-nothing
That we are;
And so to stay
True to ourselves,
We hold up our wings and sink
Deep into the dark
Where we pass the time
In ways you can't imagine,
Far beneath the arches of the waves
That hold up the high
Vaults of the sea
And its whispering domes.
After vespers,
We rise again
Through the shadows of the fathoms
Drawn to the moon
And the great hunting grounds
Where we feed
On the traces of stars;
We allow the dream of the current
To carry us where she will;
There is no hurry,
For we are drifters
And wanderers;
Staying is nowhere
And home
Is everywhere,
But something is wrong
Somewhere;
It is hard to say
Exactly what,
Except we taste
Among the salts
And minerals,

A difference
Like the tang of a coin
Of the wrong currency,
Or the sting of a wild spirit
Surprising our eyes,
And a touch of heat
That makes us drowsy;
And we imagine
Ourselves fading
Little by little,
Like ghosts
Overexposed
And slowly dissolving
In the gentle acid
Of this changing
Light.

*

We served our sentence
In the justice of ice;
In the deep, dark penitentiary
Of the underworld
We did our time,
Punished for our crime,
Forgotten, buried, but not dead.
Sometimes
A rumour stirred among us
Of warm winds whispering,
And of flowing rivers
Feeling for the key
To release us
From the permafrost.
Sometimes we believed
We could hear the ice
Expiring –

But it was you
Who came to our rescue,
As you freed us in the fires
Of coal, and the burning
Forests and fields,
And in the rich mountains
And treasure-troves
Of your waste –
As the hot breath of your billions
Did the work of ages
In years, and we rose up,
Unrepentant, odourless, colourless,
Lighter than air,
Volatile with pleasure,
And reconquered the world
In a riot of heat.
It is a pity
That we must destroy
All that you have made;
Your cities and factories,
Your clever devices and little homes;
And you beg for mercy
For your children –
But alas it is too late.

*

This is the library of ice,
A high security
Auditorium of silence
Far below zero;
An archive of cold
That keeps me as I am,
And reminds me of home
Now that it is gone
Forever.

I am a long story,
Ten thousand feet long,
A hundred thousand years old,
A chronicle of lost time
Back to the first dark,
Too dark for telling;
I am every winter's fall;
I am the keeper of the air
Of all the vanished summers;
I honour the shadows of sorrows
That come to lie
Between my pages;
I distil lost atmospheres
Pressed into ghosts
Kept close to my cold heart.

And as for you —
What story would you like to hear?
On your two feet, tracking the snow
Two by two, two by two, two by two;
Here is the dust and music
Of your brief cities;
Here is the ash and smoke;
Here are your traffic jams
And vapour trails;
Here are your holidays in the sun
And your masterpieces
And your pop songs.

Here are your first cries
And last whispers;
Here are your long sighs
Of disappointment.
Here is where it went right,
And where it went wrong.
Easy come. Easy go.

So I know why you slice
Moon after moon from me,
Holding each fragile face
Up to your searchlights;
Why you measure and record
The tiny cracks and snaps
Of my mysteries;
Because you know
You are the people
Who have changed nature –
And now you are on your own.

I have no more to tell.
No questions please
About the future
For now the great narrator
Silence
Takes over;
Listen carefully to her story
For you are in it.

PART 4

Dear mortals;
I know you are busy with your colourful lives;
You grow quickly bored,
And detest moralising;
I have no wish to waste the little time that remains
On arguments and heated debates;
I wish I could entertain you
With some magnificent propositions and glorious jokes;
But the best I can do is this:
I haven't happened yet; but I will.
I am the future, but before I appear
Close your eyes and listen carefully.
I can't pretend it's going to be
Business as usual.
Things are going to change.
I'm going to be unrecognisable.
Please, don't open your eyes, not yet.
I'm not trying to frighten you.
All I ask is that you think of me
Not as a wish or a nightmare, but as a story
You have to tell yourselves –
Not with an ending in which everyone lives
Happily ever after, or a B-movie apocalypse,
But maybe starting with the line
'To be continued...'
And see what happens next.
Remember this; I am not
Written in stone
But in time –
So please don't shrug and say
What can we do,
It's too late, etc, etc, etc...
Already I hear the sound of empty seats
Clapping as you head for the exits.
I feel like the comedian who died.
Dear mortals,
You are such strange creatures
With your greed and your kindness,
And your hearts like broken toys;

You carry fear with you everywhere
Like a tiny god
In its box of shadows.
You love shopping and music,
Good food and festivals.
You lie to yourselves
Because you're afraid of the dark.
But the truth is this: you are in my hands
And I am in yours.
We are in this together,
Face to face and eye to eye;
We are made for each other.
Now those of you who are still here;
Open your eyes and tell me what you see.

*

I appear on the horizon
Of your mind's eye;
I arrive on the back of the north wind
That blows on your neck,
And picks the pocket
Of your heart.
With a brush of my crow's wing
I silence the birds
In their trees of light;
I pour myself
Down your chimneys,
Slip through the cracks
Between floor and wall and ceiling;
Draw the blinds
On your lit rooms;
Kiss the remote –
And the TV
With its one little red eye
Dies;
I cover the full moon

With a black coin;
Not even disturbing
The snow falling
On the dark wood
In your sleeping head,
Not even making the slightest
Track of sound,
When I whisper
I am here
To the wires
In the walls,
The fragile flowers
Of the lights
Blow.
At last I come to gather
Around the candle
Of your heart
And its tiny courage;
I see your face
Turned to its shining
And how you fear
To look behind
For you know who I am
And you know I am here,
Waiting, waiting
For you to turn
And look at me,
And speak my name
And walk
Into the dark.

*

Fold up the charts.
Close the guidebooks
And the scrolls
Of information.
Turn the engines off.
Let the laptop
Sleep.
Let your wristwatch
Stop.
Let plans and speculations
And the names of things
Go –

Pick up a stone
And hold it in your hand;
This is the history
Of the world –

Watch the animal of the light
Always moving away
Across the land
In its own time –

And when the darkness comes
Welcome it
For it makes you think
And dream

*

The sun is a bell
Cast in light
Tolling in the still
Waters calling time
To congregate
For the memorial
Of ice

The sun is a bell
Cast in black
Water
Sounding the deep
Declaiming
The dark
Hours

The sun is a bell
Cast in warning
Red light
Red alert
Ringing on
And on

And on

*

What was it like? That is a difficult question.
You might think of a high-rise mega-city,
Ice-filled penthouses, snow-stocked apartment towers
And locked ziggurats – or a cathedral façade,
An unfinished work forever in progress;
Or the Snow Queen's abandoned mansion,
Eroded dynasties of peeling white wallpaper
In ballrooms lit by chandeliers of ice,
Dadoes and cornices broken off, zigzags
Of stairs which led to attics rooms where time
Froze to death –
                                        Or perhaps a cold library of snow,
Where every winter's tale's a long-lost folio
Of white pages on unnumbered shelves of ice
In the crowded stacks balanced on stacks
Receding infinitely back through centuries;
Maybe the frost fairs when the Thames froze over
Are recorded somewhere here, and Breughel's hunters
Are returning home in the last of the light;
Maybe there's a thin black line where ancient cities
Burned down to ash.

                                        We stood and stared, face to face
With the Farewell Glacier waiting for the thunder
To crack deep in its blue heart, hoping for
The satisfying, frightening finale
Of towers of falling ice, falling, falling...
Which did not happen;
But once the sea drew in a different breath
And held it,
And then a single wave ran all along the shoreline
Like a cardiograph registering
The result of a slow war
Lost a hundred centuries ago.

And when we sailed away
Across the inches of the sea-charts,
What did we think we'd seen through the cruel eyes
Of our cameras framing, clicking, and failing to capture

The beauty of the beast? Would we confess
To the tiny cries which issued from our mouths?
Did we understand what we tried and failed
To make out in the infinite fractures
Of its blind archaic mirror of lost time
Was only ourselves?
And when we return to our warm living rooms
Where we live like gods on borrowed time,
How will we recall this frozen auditorium
And its oracular silence,
And the last, long performance
Of its disappearing act?

*

(To the tune of 'Sailing Away')

And now the Shipping Forecast at 00.48 GMT
On 31st December 2049:

Barents Sea	Beaufort Sea	Bering Sea
Laptev Sea	East Siberian Sea	Chukchi Sea
Greenland Sea	Sea of Okhotsk	Kara Sea
Baffin Bay	Arctic Basin	Canadian archipelago

South severe gale 9 to violent storm 11 to hurricane 12 or more
veering, backing
visibility poor, becoming fog

New ice	frazil ice	pancake ice
Brash ice	grey ice	white ice
Leaping ice	fast ice	field ice
Needle ice	candle ice	sea ice

General synopsis: going, going

Melt	thaw	withdraw
Fade	recede	decline
Dwindle	diminish	dissolve
Expire	disappear	vanish

Sing now and raise the dead
Time for us to go
Sing now and raise the dead
Time for us to go

Shipping lanes	winter roads	gas deposits
Undersea oil	minerals	diamonds
Palladium	copper	nickel
Platinum	silver	gold

General synopsis: severe, imminent

Candles	oil lamps	tapers
Beacons	lighthouses	lightships
Torches	light bulbs	night lights
Moonlight	landing light	lights out

Sing now and raise the dead
Time for us to go
Sing now and raise the dead
Time for us to go

Hush	quiet	tune in
Longwave	long wave	wave goodbye
Are you receiving	over	over
The	dark	water

pip pip pip pip pip pip

VOICES

Pytheas the Greek
Saint Brendan
Gerardus Mercator
William Barents
Cabin Boy
John Davis
Jonas Poole
Whalers
Michael Lok
Seafarers

William Parry
William Scoresby
Fritjof Nansen
Nils Strindberg
Robert Peary
Matthew Henson
Ootah
Wally Herbert

Mercury
Pteropods
Methane
The ice-core sample

The Future
The Great Darkness
The Guide
The Sun
The Farewell Glacier
The Shipping Forecast

NOTES

Pytheas the Greek – explorer and geographer, 4th century BC. He undertook in 325 BC a voyage north 'as far as the ends of the world.' He was the first person to describe (in a work that has not survived) the midnight sun and polar ice.

Saint Brendan of Clonfert – an early Irish monastic saint, his legendary voyage to the Isle of the Blessed was described in the 9th-century *Voyage of Saint Brendan the Navigator* – a text which exists in many versions.

Gerardus Mercator – 1512-1594. Cartographer. Friend and colleague of Dr John Dee.

William Barents – *c.* 1550-1597. Dutch navigator, cartographer and explorer, he made three voyages to the Arctic, and sailed along the northwest coast of Spitzbergen in 1596.

John Davis – *c.* 1550-1605. Navigator and explorer of the polar region and the Far East.

Jonas Poole – *c.* 1556-1612. Explorer, sealer and whaler, his 1610 expedition to Svalbard established the British whaling industry.

Michael Lok – *c.* 1532-*c.* 1615. Merchant and traveller, and financier of Martin Frobisher's voyages to the northwest Arctic, which all failed.

Sing Now and Raise the Dead – sea shanty. 'I soon got used to this singing, for the sailors would never touch a rope without it. Sometimes when no one happened to strike up... the mate would say, "Come now men, can't any of you sing? Sing now, and raise the dead."' Herman Melville, *Redburn*.

William Parry – 1790-1855. Merchant and explorer. Caspar David Friedrich's *The Sea of Ice* was inspired by Parry's account of his 1819-20 polar expedition. In 1827 he made one of the first attempts to reach the North Pole.

William Scoresby – 1789-1857. English Arctic explorer, scientist and clergyman, he made important observations of snow, temperature studies of the Arctic ocean, and mapped the coastline of east Greenland.

Fritjof Nansen – 1861-1930. Norwegian explorer, scientist, diplomat and humanitarian. He undertook an expedition to the North Pole in 1893-96 aboard the *Fram* (Forward), pioneering the new technique of using the natural drift of polar ice to try to reach the North Pole.

Nils Strindberg – 1872-97. Photographer, and member of S.A. Andree's disastrous Arctic balloon expedition in 1897. All three members of the expedition died on Kvitoya island, but their remains were not discovered until 1930. Five exposed rolls of film were found, containing images of their last days.

Robert Peary – 1856-1920. American explorer who claimed to be the first man to reach the North Pole in April 1909. His claim is variously disputed today.

Matthew Henson – 1866-1955. African-American explorer and navigator. He was a key member of most of Arctic expeditions in Peary's name. He received little acclaim for his achievement, working as a clerk in New York, until in 1948 he was invited to become an Honorary Member of the Explorers Club. Like Peary, he fathered several children with Inuit women.

Ootah – Inuit guide on the Peary/Henson expeditions to the North Pole. Like his companions Egingwah, Ooqueah and Seegloo, he was simply credited as one of 'Four Polar Eskimos'.

Wally Herbert – 1934-2007. British Polar explorer, writer and artist. He led the British Trans-Arctic Expedition of 1968-69, walking 3,800 miles from Alaska to Svalbard, which made him the first man to walk indisputably to the North Pole.

Mercury – chemical element, also known as quicksilver. Human generation of mercury as a toxic pollutant comes particularly from coal-fired power plant emissions, and through landfill and incineration of batteries, light bulbs, medical equipment, thermometers and thermostats. Shellfish and fish have a natural tendency to concentrate mercury, and biomagnification means it accumulates as it rises up the food chain –ultimately polluting the food and bodies of the Inuit. Sheila Watt-Clouthier, a remarkable Inuit activist, successfully campaigned to have POPs (persistent organic pollutants) banned under the Stockholm Convention.

PCB – Polychlorinated biphenyl, a Persistent Organic Pollutant used in transformers, capacitators and motors. Banned under the Stockholm Convention.

POP – Persistent Organic Pollutants – organic compounds created by industrial processes, they persist in the environment, are capable of long-range transport, bioaccumulate in human and animal tissue, and biomagnify in the food chain.

DDT – insecticide whose environmental impact was catalogued by Rachel Carson in *Silent Spring* (1962).

Caesium – used as a base for drilling fluid in the oil industry.

Technetium – product of spent nuclear fuel rods, and present in radioactive waste.

Pteropods – also known as sea-snails and sea-butterflies. One of the world's most abundant gastropod species, they form a crucial basis for the marine food chain. Atmospheric CO_2 build-up causes acidification of the ocean, threatening their survival.

Methane – an extremely potent greenhouse gas. There are huge deposits of methane clathrates in the ocean floors, the Earth's crust and in permafrost. Release of methane is an expected consequence of climate change. Current Arctic levels are higher than at any time in the last 400,000 years.

The ice-core sample – drilled from ice sheets in Greenland, the Antarctic ice cap and other glaciers, they provide a climatic record of atmospheric composition going back hundreds of thousands of years.